DOWN THE HATCH

BY MIKE LAMBOURNE
ILLUSTRATIONS BY THOMPSON YARDLEY

DOWN THE HATCH

THE MILLBROOK PRESS · BROOKFIELD, CONNECTICUT

Library of Congress Cataloging-in-Publication Data

Lambourne, Mike.
Down the hatch : find out about your food / by Michael Lambourne ;
illustrations by Thompson Yardley.
p.   cm.—(Lighter look book)
Includes bibliographical references and index.
Summary: Introduces the basics of nutrition and explains how
digestion works to help the body use the food it has consumed.
ISBN 1-56294-150-X
1. Digestion—Juvenile literature.   2. Nutrition—Juvenile
literature.   [1. Nutrition. 2. Digestion.] I. Yardley, Thompson,
1951–   ill. II. Title. III. Series.
QP145.L26 1992
612.3—dc20   91-22686 CIP AC

First published in the United States in 1992 by
The Millbrook Press Inc.
2 Old New Milford Road
Brookfield, Connecticut 06804
© Copyright Cassell plc 1991
First published in Great Britain in 1991 by
Cassell Publishers Limited
5 4 3 2 1

"YOU ARE WHAT YOU EAT"

So what happens if you eat too many bananas?
Will you turn into one?

No! But you'd probably be sick!
Your body needs lots of different sorts of foods
to make it grow properly. So you need to know
how to feed your body. Be a food expert!

FIND OUT . . .

What it's like to be eaten!
How food builds your body!
Why farmers spread muck!
Where cornflakes come from!

WHAT'S YOUR FAVORITE FOOD?

Ask your friends what their favorite food is.
You'll get all sorts of different answers . . .

BRR!!

CHILI BEANS!

SCRAMBLED EGGS!

GOLD

CHICKEN NUGGETS!

KOFF!!

SMOKED FISH!

SHEPHERD'S PIE!

Boring old ice-cream again!

Boring old giant hamburger again!

Everybody has a slightly different sense of taste. So not everybody likes the same things. And if you ate your favorite food all the time, you'd soon get tired of it!

Some creatures do!

Cattle stand in the grass they eat!

Some termites live in the wood they eat!

Bacteria can feed inside grass, wood, or in animals' bodies!

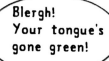

Blergh! Your tongue's gone green!

Blergh! Your tongue's gone splintery!

If other creatures can eat grass and wood, why can't people? For the answer, you have to go millions of years back in time!

MEALTIME!

All plants and animals need food and water to live and grow. The history of living things is all about finding food and having babies!

3.5 billion years ago . . . BLOBS!

Many scientists think that the first life-forms were tiny blobs, a bit like present-day bacteria. They lived in seawater and ate chemicals. Some of them grouped together and ate the smaller blobs.

2 billion years ago . . . WORMS!

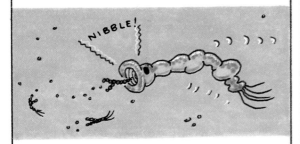

Some of these creatures developed into wriggly, wormlike animals. They could move about and eat the blobs.

570 million years ago . . . CRUSTACEANS!

Over the years, different creatures appeared. Some had legs and hard outer skeletons. They ate worms, plants, and other animals.

395 million years ago . . . FISH!

Other types of animals appeared. They had legs shaped like fins so they could swim. They could travel a long way to find food.

360 million years ago . . . AMPHIBIANS!

Some fish fed near the shore. Some had babies that could breathe air. These crawled onto the land to find food.

By this time there were millions of different sorts of plants and animals. Each became used to its own sort of food. Termites managed to live on wood. Other animals ate ferns or seaweed. Other animals ate animals!..

225 million years ago . . . DINOSAURS!

Some animals began to live on land all the time. Dinosaurs lived in warm places where there was lots of food.

65 million years ago . . . MAMMALS!

Small mammals appeared. Being hairy, they could live in colder places where there was less food. They ate whatever they could find. They came to depend on eating lots of different types of foods.

2 million years ago . . . PEOPLE!

Mammals very much like modern people gradually spread all over the world. They lived by hunting animals and gathering a wide variety of plant food.

10,000 years ago . . .
FARMING PEOPLE!

People invented farming. That meant they didn't have to search for food. But their bodies still needed variety. They raised the wild plants and animals that they were used to eating.

NOW . . . CORNFLAKES PEOPLE!

We still need a variety of foods. These days we can turn these same crops into a huge selection of attractive foods. For instance, we can turn corn into cornflakes!

Corn   Cornflakes factory   Cornflakes

STORE-BOUGHT FOOD

Nowadays you don't have to hunt for food. You can buy most of the things you want at a store.

Packages on supermarket shelves often have pictures of tasty-looking food on them. It's easy to be tempted into eating food you don't really need.

PICKING AND CHOOSING FACT

Fortunately, most people have a built-in sense of what their bodies need. Scientists once tried an experiment with children. Over a few weeks they let them eat whatever they wanted. Most of the children chose a variety of food and stayed healthy.

A MEAL WITH A GOOD VARIETY OF FOODS IS CALLED A **BALANCED MEAL**

All the food you regularly eat is called your diet. When your diet includes everything your body needs in the right amounts, it's called a balanced diet.

HOW TO CHOOSE A BALANCED DIET

Growing people should eat the following number of servings from each of these groups every day . . .

You don't need to eat huge servings of each type of food. A serving is an amount that you feel comfortable with. You also need to have fats and oils in your diet. You get these from several of the foods in the different food groups. But you should not eat too many fatty foods. You should not have more than one ounce (30 grams) of fat daily. What's so special about these foods anyway?

WHAT'S IN THEM?? . . .

Two or more glasses of milk

Milk products

Poultry   Nuts
Fish   Peas
Red meat   Beans
Eggs
           Two servings

Bread
Cereals

Three servings

Fresh fruits
Fresh vegetables

Four servings

WHAT'S IN A HAMBURGER?

There are seven main things in food, and you need them all. Remember that your body is made of the things you eat!

YOUR BODY NEEDS . . .

Here's a hamburger. It might taste good, but does it contain everything you need?

PROTEINS

Proteins are complicated chemicals that help to build muscles and skin. There are twenty-two different types of proteins. Your body can make twelve of them. The rest of them have to be in your food.

The burger contains lots of protein.

SUGARS

You need these to give your muscles energy to work. Starch and carbohydrates are complicated forms of sugar that are found in food. Your body can turn these into sugar.

The bun has lots of starch, which can be turned into sugar.

FATS

If you eat more protein or sugar than your body needs, it's stored under your skin as fat. Fat in your food is stored for later use too. Fat also makes up part of your muscles. A layer of fat under your skin keeps you warm.

There's lots of fat in the meat.

... AND WHAT'S NOT!

MINERALS

There are about twenty different minerals that food experts know are needed in food. For example, calcium and phosphorus help to make bones. Iron keeps your blood healthy, and so on.

There are usually enough minerals in a hamburger.

VITAMINS

These are chemicals that help your body function. Vitamins are found in most fresh foods. Spinach has vitamin A, whole wheat bread has vitamin B, cauliflower has vitamin C, and so on. There are over a dozen vitamins.

Hamburgers don't have a good variety of vitamins. Add a salad!

FIBER

Fiber helps your intestines push food through your body. Cereals, vegetables, and fruits are partly made of fiber.

Hamburgers don't have enough fiber. Add an apple!

WATER

About two thirds of your body is water. You need to keep on replacing water as you lose it through breathing, going to the toilet, and sweating. All these things added together make a BALANCED MEAL!

Hamburgers don't have enough water. Add some orange juice ...

HUNGER

If you don't eat a balanced diet, you'll become ill. That's your body's way of telling you to change your eating habits! You could live on cookies and lemonade for a few weeks before you started feeling poorly. Your body can store some of the vitamins and minerals it needs.

Sugar is also stored in your blood. This gives you about six hours of energy for your muscles. Even sitting and reading takes energy. Your brain needs sugar too!

Your liver stores sugar after a meal. And your pancreas controls the flow of sugar through your blood vessels to your brain and muscles.

As your sugar becomes used up, you start to feel tired and hungry. Your liver tells your brain that it's running out of sugar. Then your brain tells your body to eat!

INSIDE A BLOOD VESSEL . . .

BYE BYE!

I'm going to the legs!

I'm going to be sweat!

BYE BYE!

Your blood carries the proteins, sugars, fats, minerals, vitamins, and water from your food and drink. Blood has to contain the right amount of each chemical for your body to work properly.

When you get hot, you sweat. If you sweat, your body loses water. That means you don't have the right balance of chemicals and water in your blood. Your brain tells you that you're thirsty and you go and get a drink.

I'm still thirsty!

So buy another can!

A lot of people reach for a drink of fizzy soda when they are thirsty. It may taste good—and it's certainly sweet. A can of soda might contain about eight teaspoons of sugar! But soda may not get rid of your thirst very well. And it can leave a sticky feeling in your mouth. Try a glass of plain cold water and see if that works better next time you're thirsty.

Now that you know that food and drink are made out of chemicals, find out . . . WHAT'S IN CHEMICALS!

[15]

WHAT'S IN CHEMICALS?

Everything in the universe is made up of tiny particles called atoms. They are far too small to see, even with a microscope!

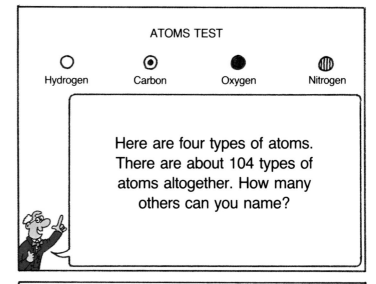

ATOMS TEST

Hydrogen   Carbon   Oxygen   Nitrogen

Here are four types of atoms. There are about 104 types of atoms altogether. How many others can you name?

Sometimes atoms stick together. Two or more atoms stuck together form a molecule. Hydrogen and oxygen stuck together make a molecule of water.

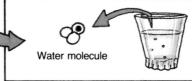

Water molecule

There are billions of molecules in a glass of water.

Sugar molecule

Sugar cube

Food is made of billions of molecules too. But they're usually very complicated.

Strings of sugar molecules

Bread

Starchy foods such as bread are made of strings of sugar molecules stuck together.

And protein and fat molecules are even more complicated!

Protein molecule

Chicken

In fact, protein, fat, and starch molecules are so big and complicated that our bodies can't even use them as they are.

Even though many food molecules are too big for our bodies to use, they're actually very tiny. They're bigger than atoms, but they're still too small to see. So . . . it's no good trying to chop them up with a knife and fork!

Fortunately, your body produces an army of chemicals that can break down food molecules!

As soon as you put food in your mouth, it starts to be broken down.

This process is called DIGESTION . . .

DOWN THE HATCH!

Digestion begins in your mouth . . .

Food is often too big to swallow whole. So you take bites out of it with your teeth.

Then you chew the bitten-off piece. As you chew, the inside of your mouth dribbles out wet stuff called saliva. Your bite of food turns into a slippy, sloppy ball of food.

I'm a bite of sandwich!

WOW! I'm being chewed!

ERK! LICK! SALIVA

Now I'm a slippy, sloppy ball of food!

ERK!

GULP!

BULGE!

SLIPPY SLOPPY SALIVA FACT

Saliva contains water and a chemical called an enzyme. This starts to break down the sugar in the ball of food. And . . . the wet saliva makes it easier for you to swallow. So give your food a good chewing before you swallow it!

There's this thing in your mouth, too . . .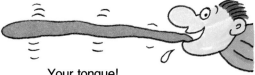

Your tongue!

WHAT YOUR TONGUE DOES

You need your tongue to be able to talk. But try not to do it while you're eating!

THRRP! GAB GAB! FLOBB! FOO! NATTER! DRIBBLE! FOO!

You can taste food with your tongue. Your sense of taste is very important. It lets you know if food is all right to eat before you swallow it.

A TONGUE

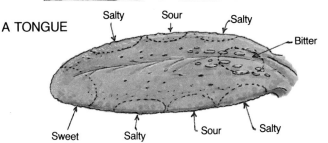

Salty   Sour   Salty
Bitter
Sweet   Salty   Sour   Salty

Your sense of smell is connected to your sense of taste. Try this and see.

1. Put on a blindfold.
2. Hold your nose so that you can't smell anything. Try not to cheat!
3. Now see if you can tell the difference between a selection of fruits. Try other sorts of food, too.

Hmm nice! It tastes like a peach!

I'm glad it's not a pear! I hate pears!

Pear

Your tongue moves your food around your mouth. This lets all of your teeth get to work on it. When you've finished chewing, the back of your tongue pushes the food ball down your throat.

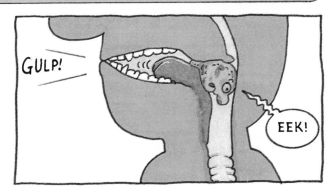

GULP!

EEK!

INTO YOUR TUMMY

The food ball travels down a tube of muscles called the esophagus. The muscles squeeze the food ball down to your stomach.

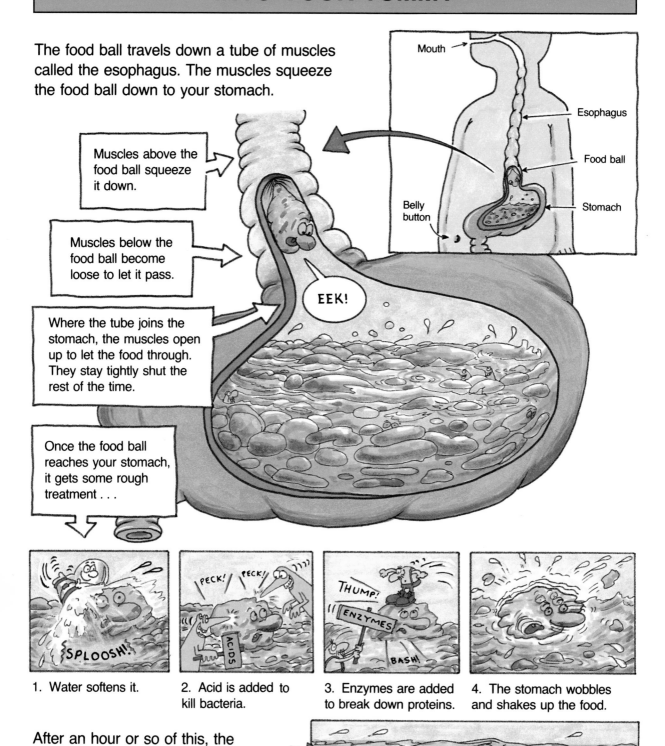

Mouth

Esophagus

Food ball

Belly button

Stomach

Muscles above the food ball squeeze it down.

Muscles below the food ball become loose to let it pass.

Where the tube joins the stomach, the muscles open up to let the food through. They stay tightly shut the rest of the time.

EEK!

Once the food ball reaches your stomach, it gets some rough treatment . . .

1. Water softens it. SPLOOSH!

2. Acid is added to kill bacteria. PECK! PECK! ACIDS

3. Enzymes are added to break down proteins. THUMP! ENZYMES BASH!

4. The stomach wobbles and shakes up the food.

After an hour or so of this, the food balls become a lumpy puddle!

Missing meals or eating at odd times can trick your stomach. Then it may start to prepare for a meal that doesn't arrive! Acid and enzymes are waiting to break down food protein. But your stomach is also made of protein!

HEY! Your watch must have stopped. It's time for lunch!

Too much acid wears away the stomach walls. Sometimes you can feel this. It's called indigestion! It's best to eat at regular times. Then your stomach knows when to produce digestive acid.

Sometimes, you may eat things that your stomach doesn't like. Then your stomach muscles squeeze your food back up the esophagus. Then you're sick!

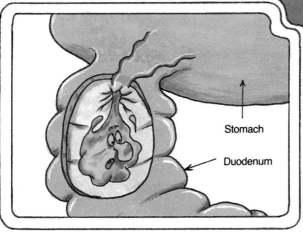

The stomach's job is to store and prepare food for the next part of its journey. When the food is mixed, it's squirted into your duodenum. This is the first part of your intestines.

DOWN THE TUBE

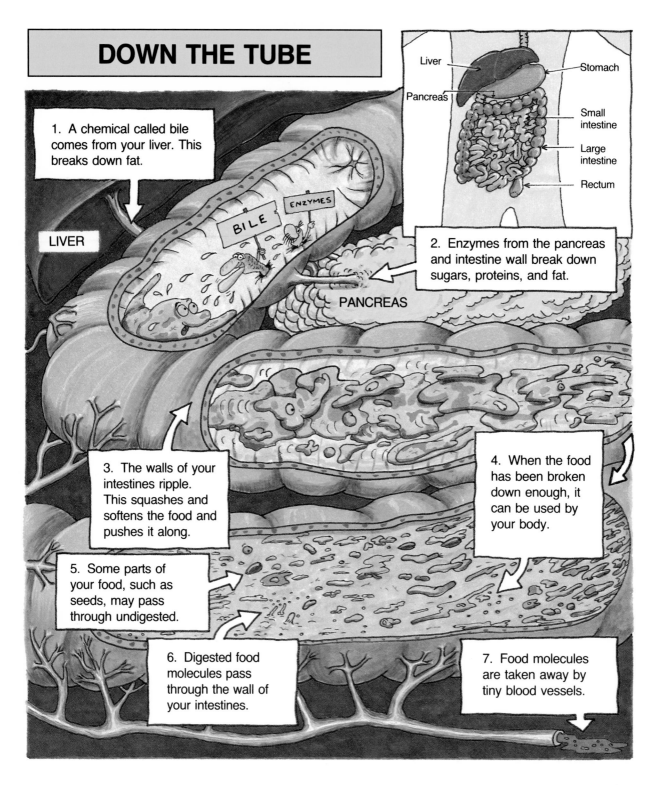

1. A chemical called bile comes from your liver. This breaks down fat.

LIVER

BILE

ENZYMES

Liver
Pancreas
Stomach
Small intestine
Large intestine
Rectum

2. Enzymes from the pancreas and intestine wall break down sugars, proteins, and fat.

PANCREAS

3. The walls of your intestines ripple. This squashes and softens the food and pushes it along.

4. When the food has been broken down enough, it can be used by your body.

5. Some parts of your food, such as seeds, may pass through undigested.

6. Digested food molecules pass through the wall of your intestines.

7. Food molecules are taken away by tiny blood vessels.

This part of your digestive system is called the small intestine. It takes most of the useful materials out of your food.

The small intestine is connected to the large intestine. This takes water from the unused food material.

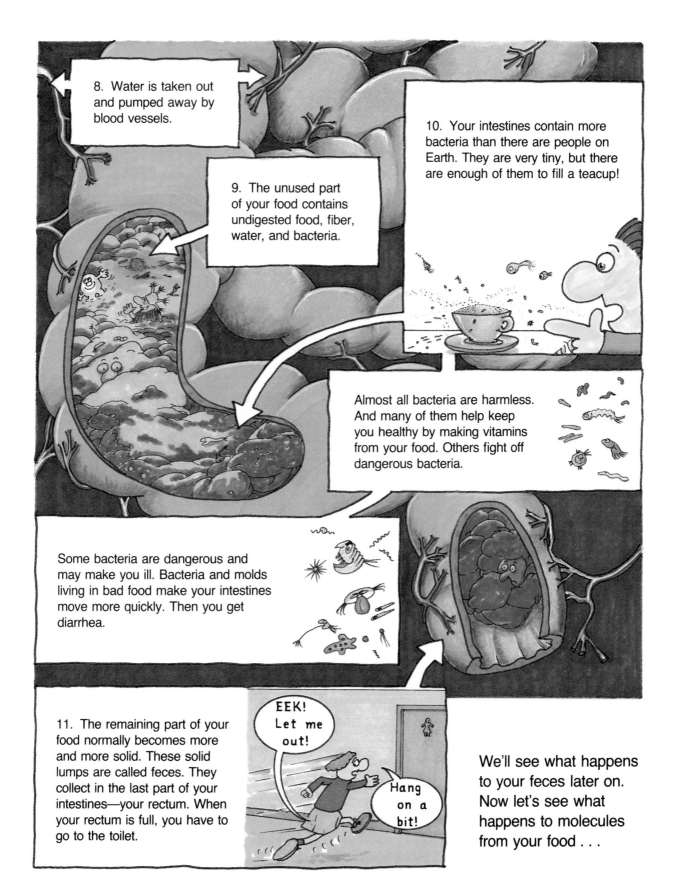

8. Water is taken out and pumped away by blood vessels.

9. The unused part of your food contains undigested food, fiber, water, and bacteria.

10. Your intestines contain more bacteria than there are people on Earth. They are very tiny, but there are enough of them to fill a teacup!

Almost all bacteria are harmless. And many of them help keep you healthy by making vitamins from your food. Others fight off dangerous bacteria.

Some bacteria are dangerous and may make you ill. Bacteria and molds living in bad food make your intestines move more quickly. Then you get diarrhea.

11. The remaining part of your food normally becomes more and more solid. These solid lumps are called feces. They collect in the last part of your intestines—your rectum. When your rectum is full, you have to go to the toilet.

EEK! Let me out!

Hang on a bit!

We'll see what happens to your feces later on. Now let's see what happens to molecules from your food . . .

[23]

THE EATING GAME (FOR TWO TO SIX PLAYERS)

HOW TO PLAY . . .

1. Each player pretends to be a healthy chunk of food.

2. Write your name and ingredients on a card, as pictured below.

3. Decide who will start.

4. Roll dice to move your counter along the squares.

5. You can move in any direction during a move except backward. You can move backward after reaching a dead end.

6. Cross off the words on your card as you land on places to deliver your ingredients.

7. You can deliver the first seven ingredients in any order.

8. The first player to cross off the first seven ingredients and take the waste to the toilet is the winner!

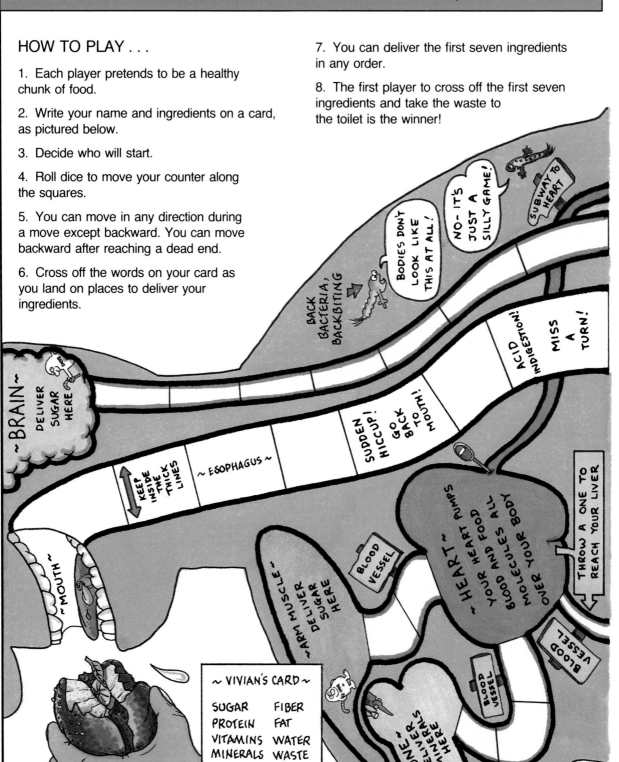

BACK BACTERIA, BACKBITING

BODIES DON'T LOOK LIKE THIS AT ALL!

NO- IT'S JUST A SILLY GAME!

SUBWAY TO HEART

ACID INDIGESTION!

MISS A TURN!

~BRAIN~ DELIVER SUGAR HERE

KEEP INSIDE THE THICK LINES

~ESOPHAGUS~

SUDDEN HICCUP! GO BACK TO MOUTH!

THROW A ONE TO REACH YOUR LIVER

~MOUTH~

~ARM MUSCLE~ DELIVER SUGAR HERE

BLOOD VESSEL

~HEART~ YOUR HEART PUMPS BLOOD AND FOOD MOLECULES ALL OVER YOUR BODY

BLOOD VESSEL

BLOOD VESSEL

~VIVIAN'S CARD~

SUGAR	FIBER
PROTEIN	FAT
VITAMINS	WATER
MINERALS	WASTE

~BONE~ DELIVERS MINERA HERE

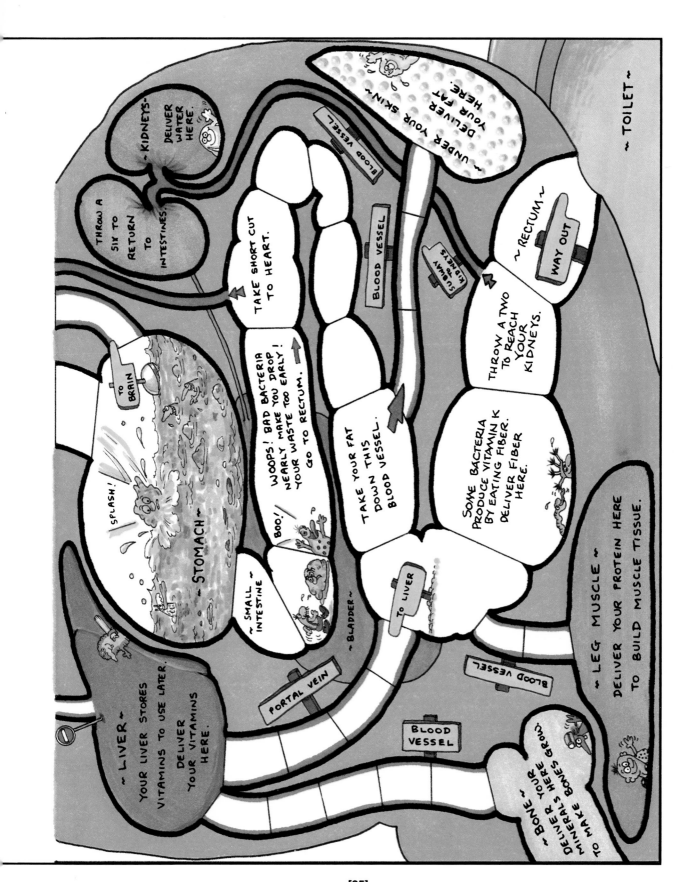

THE FOOD CYCLE

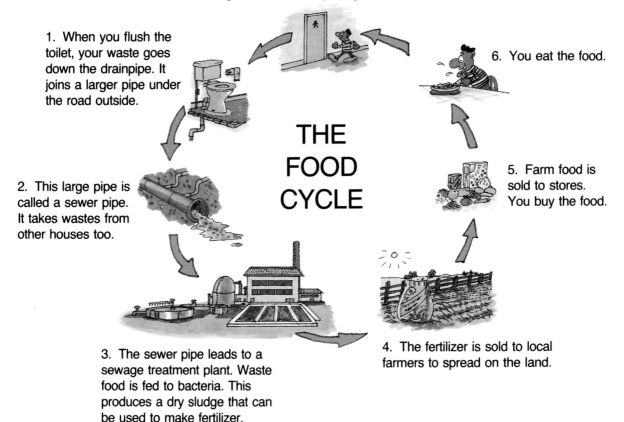

7. Your body uses up the food. You go to the toilet to pass your waste.

1. When you flush the toilet, your waste goes down the drainpipe. It joins a larger pipe under the road outside.

6. You eat the food.

5. Farm food is sold to stores. You buy the food.

2. This large pipe is called a sewer pipe. It takes wastes from other houses too.

3. The sewer pipe leads to a sewage treatment plant. Waste food is fed to bacteria. This produces a dry sludge that can be used to make fertilizer.

4. The fertilizer is sold to local farmers to spread on the land.

Animals take part in food cycles too.
Cowpats turn into cow food after a few weeks!

1. A cow drops a cowpat.

2. Flies, beetles, and bacteria feed on the cowpat and break it down.

3. Fungi grow up and die away. This also helps to break down the cowpat.

6. A cow comes along and eats the new grass.

5. Grass seeds feed on the food molecules and grow into plants.

4. Rain falls. The broken-down food molecules soak into the ground.

You can see this working with plants of your own. Tell your parents what you're doing first!

MAKE YOUR OWN FERTILIZER . . .

1. Fill two flowerpots with clean sand. Plant a bean seed an inch (2.5 centimeters) deep in each pot. Add some water and put them in the sunlight.

2. Get some horse manure, or buy a small bag of composted manure from a garden-supply store.

3. Put the manure in a cloth bag and put it in a bucket of water. Food chemicals will soak into the water.

4. Both plants will start to grow if you keep the sand damp.

5. Water one plant with tap water. Water the other with water from the bucket.

6. After a few weeks you'll see that the bucket-fed plant looks healthier than the other one!

STUCK-IN-MUCK FACT

Some farmers collect the manure from farm animals. They spread it on their land to help the plants to grow. This is called muck-spreading or manuring.

What's for dinner, Mom?

BOILED SOIL!

Soil is very important. Apart from seafood, everything we eat comes from the soil. But we can't eat soil!

Instead, we grow plants that change soil chemicals into food. If the soil chemicals run out, the soil becomes useless for growing crops. Plants won't grow properly in this tired soil. Many farmers in poor countries can't afford fertilizers to help their plants. Sometimes their soil becomes so weak that it turns into desert!

Farm and ranch animals use up soil too, especially when farmers don't use manure to keep the soil healthy. In fact, it takes a lot more soil to raise farm and ranch animals than it does to grow crops . . .

WHAT-MEAT-REALLY-COSTS FACT

Piece of meat from a cow feeds one person
The land taken up by a cow could feed five to ten people!

Cattle have to eat at least 100 tons of plants to produce 10 tons of beef. So meat costs a lot more than the same amount of food in plant form.

NO MEAT ON THE MENU

Vegetarians are people who choose not to eat meat at all. Some people don't eat meat for medical reasons or because they don't believe in killing animals for food. Some religions don't allow meat eating. Most vegetarians will eat animal products such as cheese. But vegans are very strict vegetarians. Some vegans won't use anything that came from an animal.

You may decide to become a vegetarian. Be careful! Growing people need lots of vitamins, proteins, and minerals. Strict vegetarians need to take special vitamin pills to make up for not eating meat. If you don't want to take pills, you need meat and animal products to stay healthy.

Farmers in South America are cutting down large areas of forests to make way for cattle. Some of these forests produce fruit and nuts we could eat instead of beef. The less beef we eat, the fewer trees we have to cut down!

FAT FACTS

Everybody knows what happens when you eat a big meal—your belly sticks out!

Where most fat is stored . . .

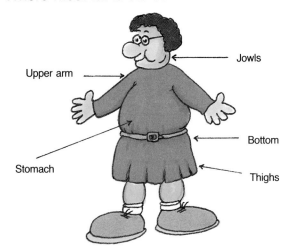

Jowls

Upper arm

Bottom

Stomach

Thighs

That's because your stomach swells up to hold the food. But if you keep on eating big meals, the rest of your body may swell up too! Your body stores unused energy from your food. Then you get fat!

Hairs

Outer skin

Blood vessels

Fat globules

Fat people have bodies that are just too good at storing energy. Some people's bodies become fat even when they eat only small meals! But they are often thought of as being greedy or lazy. This makes them very upset. Once people have gained a lot of weight, it's hard for them to lose it again.

How would YOU like to be made fun of?

On the other hand, some people are as thin as a board! That's not always because they don't eat much. It's just that their bodies aren't storing the energy from their food. Some people eat a lot and still stay thin.

Other people try all sorts of ways to lose weight. Some people even try to become slim by secretly making themselves throw up. This is very dangerous. It damages the stomach and the esophagus, and it also wastes the water, minerals, and vitamins the body needs. And it makes a mess!

Growing people need to be especially careful about dieting. They should take their parents' or doctor's advice first.

Exercising and eating properly are the best ways to keep healthy and trim.

Mom and Dad's special training run!

That's because bacteria like to eat your food too! Along with fungi, bacteria make your food go bad. Using cans, vacuum packs, and refrigerators are the usual ways to protect food. Once you open a package of food, you have to fight bacteria.

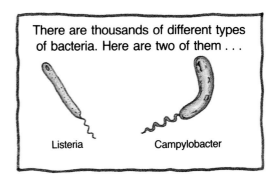

There are thousands of different types of bacteria. Here are two of them . . .

Listeria   Campylobacter

Bacteria need three things to live . . .

1. FOOD

Leaving crumbs and leftovers around after eating encourages bacteria to grow.

2. WATER

Bacteria like living in damp dishcloths and sponges and on wet surfaces. Keeping things dry helps to keep out bacteria.

3. WARMTH

Bacteria enjoy warm places but can't stand too much heat. Hot soapy water kills most bacteria. And bacteria can't grow in cold places. But some refrigerators just aren't cold enough.

Always clean up after spilling food.

Check your refrigerator with a thermometer. It should read no more than 39°F (4°C).

Some chilled or fresh food goes bad quite quickly. It's against the law to sell products after the "USE BY" date.

And selling products after the "BEST BEFORE" date is against the law. Products with this label stay edible for a long time but go bad eventually.

INGREDIENTS LABELS

Food companies often add chemicals to food. These are called additives . . .

Preservatives stop food from going bad. Flavoring gives bland food a stronger taste. Coloring gives pale food an attractive color.

Food companies use hundreds of different additives. Their use is controlled by law, and most of them are harmless. But some people are badly affected by food additives and become ill.

You may want to avoid foods that are full of additives. So . . . check out product labels before you buy!

[33]

COOKING

PROCESSED FOOD
Food that you buy in packages has often been processed. This means that it's been through a factory process such as cooking or baking. Some factory processing removes vitamins and minerals from food.

FRESH FOOD
Most fresh food hasn't been processed. So eating fresh food gives you the vitamins and minerals that processed food often lacks.

Fresh fruits and vegetables don't usually contain preservatives. So eat them before too many bacteria arrive.

Bacteria can't stand too much heat!

But we need to cook some foods. For example, steaming softens potatoes and corn on the cob so they can be digested more easily. Raw meat is usually too tough to eat. And cooking kills off the bacteria that live in meat products.

But watch out! Overcooking ruins fresh food. If vegetables are boiled for too long, most of the goodness ends up in the water!

... AND EATING

Why not learn how to cook for yourself?
Then you'll know what's in your food!
Find out about cooking simple meals
from your parents. Then you can
invite your friends to dinner.
Make up a crazy menu like
this and pretend that it's
what they'll be eating!

ERMINTRUDE'S
RESTAURANT
~ MENU ~
STARTERS
SARDINES AND CUSTARD
BREAD AND SALT
VINEGAR AND ICE-CREAM
LETTUCE AND MARMALADE
MUSTARD MILK-SHAKE
MAIN MEALS
TOASTED SHEEP'S EYEBALLS
CURRIED STRAWBERRIES
FRIED JAM ON HERRINGS
(WITH REAL LARD!)
BOILED CABBAG
BAKED

What's this garbage?

I can't eat this!

Yuck!

I'm going home!

I'm telling my mom on you - you're nuts!

EEKi

If you're eating out, it's sometimes harder to stick to a
healthy diet. Food experts work out balanced school
meals. But it's up to you to make the right choices!

SCHOOL CANTEEN

I only eat fries!

FAST-FOOD FACT

McBLOGGS' CHIKKIN-FRIES

Fast-food
restaurants don't
always give you the
choice of a proper
meal. Check out the
menu before you
choose a snack.

Who's that?

It's crazy Charlie! He only eats fries!

Fries are good for you!

Yes - but not all the time!!!

Tired brain

Bad skin

Tired legs

Fat stomach

[35]

Now that you know food makes you grow you can find out by how much. CHECK YOUR HEIGHT! Put a pencil line on your bedroom doorjamb to mark your present height. Add new lines every month to see how you're growing up!

Eat a good variety of foods, but . . .

DON'T EAT THIS BOOK!

Only bookworms eat books!

FIND OUT MORE

Now that you've learned about your food and what becomes of it, you may want to find out more about nutrition and digestion. Here are some books to look for in the library.

Food and Digestion, by Steve Parker (Watts, 1990)

How Our Bodies Work: Food and Digestion, by Jan Burgess (Silver Burdett, 1988)

What Happens to a Hamburger?, by Paul Showers (Harper Jr., 1985)

Your Stomach and Digestive Tract, by Herbert S. Zim (Morrow, 1973)

INDEX